AI Powered HR:

An In-Depth Guide to ChatGPT for Human Resources Professionals

MATT DUNN

Copyright © 2024 Author Name

All rights reserved.

CONTENTS

1	Introduction	1
2	A Brief History of ChatGPT	3
3	How to Use ChatGPT	8
4	Before You Get Started	13
5	Use Cases of ChatGPT in HR	17
	Use Case 1 - Recruitment	19
	Use Case 2 - Onboarding	30
	Use Case 3 - Performance Management	37
	Use Case 4 - Learning and Development	54
	Use Case 5 – Policy Development and Refinement	73
6	The Risks of Using ChatGPT (and how to combat them)	77
	Epilogue	81
	Appendix – ChatGPT Free versus ChatGPT Plus	82

1 INTRODUCTION

Welcome to "The ChatGPT HR Advantage: Mastering the AI Revolution in HR". Your journey through this book will reveal the extraordinary opportunities awaiting HR professionals ready to harness the power of AI, particularly the potential of ChatGPT.

The tale begins back in 1987, when I'd saved up to buy my first computer. As a child, my fingers danced across a ZX Spectrum keyboard, lighting up my imagination with the possibilities of programming. During this era, Lotus 1-2-3 was a cutting-edge spreadsheet tool, hinting at the future omnipresence of sophisticated data tools..

I stepped further into the digital realm at Rhodes University, where the untapped potential of the internet and the tantalising prospect of remote work (a concept that, although feasible at the time, only became a widespread reality after the global pandemic in 2020) came into my purview. In 1999, my first mobile phone rang, ushering me into an era of constant connectivity.

While working at the International Data Corporation, I used technology to morph a week-long task into a few short hours by writing Excel macros, illustrating the power of software to optimise operations. This experience thrust me into the unfolding narrative of mobile devices. Here, I encountered the XDA, a forebear of today's smartphones, and the iPod, a device that would redefine our interaction with music.

In 2007, I held my first iPhone. The sleek device in my palm hinted at a paradigm shift in personal technology. A decade later, the world of Robotic Process Automation (RPA) opened up before me, during a conversation at a KPMG dinner. This encounter led to co-founding a company dedicated to transforming the way businesses operate through process automation.

In 2022, I began exploring AI writing assistants. Discovering these potent tools was akin to a close encounter with a new species of intelligence, the likes of which humankind had never seen. This was my introduction to ChatGPT, a form of generative AI that I immediately recognised as a game-changer, a catalyst on par with the advent of computers, spreadsheets, the internet, and mobile technology.

HR professionals are now at the forefront of an exciting new era, where AI and human resources intersect. Navigating this transformation will be crucial for professionals to stand out.

The promise and warning are clear: **AI won't replace HR professionals, but those who can leverage AI might replace those who cannot.**

This book does more than just help you understand this powerful tool. It equips you with practical strategies to leverage AI in HR, keeping you ahead in a rapidly evolving technological landscape.

Drawing on my extensive experience in management consulting and technology, I will guide you through this exciting journey. "The ChatGPT HR Advantage" is your roadmap to integrating AI into HR, from recruitment to employee engagement and performance management, streamlining processes, cutting costs, and boosting decision-making.

Whether you're an HR leader, team member, or handle HR tasks in a smaller organisation, this book will enhance your performance, increase efficiency, and save time.

WHY? As HR professionals and custodians of your organisation's evolving skillset requirements, it's crucial to become well-versed in this technology for both your existing workforce and the recruitment of new entrants.

Thank you for joining me on this voyage. Now, let's dive into the future of HR and unveil the promise of AI.

2 A BRIEF HISTORY OF CHATGPT

In this chapter, you will learn:

- The timeline of AI from its inception to the present day, including the emergence of deep learning and the recent advancements in AI models like ChatGPT.

- OpenAI's contribution to the field of AI and its development of ChatGPT, a powerful AI model trained on vast amounts of internet data.

- The capabilities of ChatGPT, including its extensive knowledge base and its ability to understand and sustain intelligent dialogues.

- The practical applications of ChatGPT in the HR function, such as resume screening, candidate engagement, onboarding, training and development, and performance management.

- The benefits of using ChatGPT in HR, including improved efficiency, time savings, and enhanced service to employees, allowing HR professionals to focus on more strategic activities.

The Evolution of AI: A Timeline

Artificial Intelligence (AI) has fascinated us for centuries, but its serious pursuit began in the mid-20th century. Our journey starts in 1956 at Dartmouth College, where brilliant minds first formally explored the concept of 'intelligent machines.

In the following decades, innovative algorithms and techniques significantly advanced AI. The 1980s, however, proved pivotal with the emergence of 'deep learning,' a technique crafted by John Hopfield and David Rumelhart. It employed artificial neural networks to learn from data and became the foundation of myriad AI applications, ranging from image recognition to speech recognition.

Recently, interest in AI has surged, driven by models like OpenAI's ChatGPT, which are trained on vast datasets. Capable of generating text, translating languages, and delivering informative responses, ChatGPT showcases AI's evolving capabilities.

AI permeates our lives, revolutionising medicine, driving autonomous vehicle development, composing music and more recently generating video content (search for "SORA" to find out more). As we stand on the brink of this AI revolution, it's clear that it's poised to reshape our future, including business, in ways unimaginable.

OpenAI's Contribution:

Founded in 2015, OpenAI's notable initial members included Elon Musk, Sam Altman, and Ilya Sutskever, among other AI luminaries.

OpenAI's goal was to ensure that artificial general intelligence benefits all of humanity. OpenAI has launched impressive projects like DALL-E and Whisper, but this book focuses on their standout achievement, the Generative Pre-trained Transformer (GPT). GPT is an AI model that OpenAI started developing in 2016. Over the next five years, OpenAI refined GPT by training it on a vast amount of internet data.

ChatGPT:

In 2022, OpenAI unveiled ChatGPT, a significant development in AI chatbots that enhanced natural language processing. This advancement attracted a substantial $11 billion investment from Microsoft, significantly enhancing ChatGPT's capabilities.

ChatGPT was trained using a diverse and vast dataset from the internet, including billions of sentences from webpages, academic texts, and social media, creating a large repository of human knowledge.

ChatGPT is a sophisticated AI that crafts detailed responses by predicting words through statistical analysis, demonstrating AI's potential to transform businesses.

ChatGPT features two key aspects:

Knowledge: a vast data library from its training that enables it to respond to numerous queries; and
Understanding: the capacity to emulate comprehension, allowing it to interpret, analyse, and maintain intelligent dialogues.

Globally, millions use ChatGPT for various applications:
- engaging in lifelike conversations,
- providing detailed answers,
- creating diverse textual content like poems and scripts, and
- effectively translating languages.

The launch of ChatGPT stirred the tech industry, prompting Google to develop Bard. A mishap during Bard's demo led to a 7% drop in Google's shares, costing about $100 billion, while Microsoft's shares rose, highlighting the recognised potential of such technology.

If ChatGPT can directly answer user queries, it could revolutionise information search, currently dominated by Google.

Since the first edition, I've trained over 2,000 business users on effective and responsible ChatGPT usage, incorporating their feedback and findings into this updated version.

You can reach ChatGPT via your browser by going to this URL: https://chat.openai.com where you can sign up for a free account which I'd suggest doing before continuing onto the next chapter.

Once you've had a chance to play and experiment with ChatGPT, you may wish to consider upgrading to ChatGPT Plus. You can see what the differences are in the appendix at the end of this book.

Why ChatGPT is relevant to HR professionals

HR professionals use ChatGPT to enhance tasks such as:

- Recruitment—screening resumes and scheduling interviews—freeing them for strategic activities

- Onboarding by informing new hires about company policies, boosting their confidence.

- Training, it helps develop personalised programs, enhancing employee skills crucial for their roles.

- Performance management by analysing feedback and offering development coaching.

ChatGPT is invaluable for HR professionals, enhancing efficiency, saving time, and improving employee services. It allows HR to focus on more rewarding aspects of their roles, such as strategic planning rather than routine tasks like writing policies.

Chapter Summary/Key Takeaways

- OpenAI's ChatGPT is an AI-based chatbot that allows anyone to interact with it easily, developed by feeding it with extensive internet data to enhance its language prediction ability.

- ChatGPT can construct sentences based on the context of its given prompts and identify the most probable next word using statistical analysis based on its training data.

- The release of ChatGPT created a buzz in the tech industry, leading to Google's creation of its version, called "Bard."

- ChatGPT has the potential to revolutionise how we search for information and streamline the recruitment process for HR professionals, providing comprehensive support throughout the entire employee onboarding process.

In the next chapter you will learn all about how to use ChatGPT.

3 HOW TO USE CHATGPT

In this chapter, you will learn:

- How ChatGPT, an AI tool, creates personalised, human-like answers.
- The various tasks ChatGPT can do, such as:

    o   Making content from prompts,
    o   Improving responses using extra questions,
    o   Summarising and refining existing content, and
    o   Comparing different pieces of information.

- The need to ask clear questions for useful answers from ChatGPT.
- How ChatGPT keeps track of conversation topics.
- How to use ChatGPT's user-friendly interface for chatting, saving conversations, and reviewing past chats.
- The value of trying out different prompts to understand what ChatGPT can do.

ChatGPT is a clever AI tool that talks like a very well-informed human. It doesn't use ready-made answers like other chatbots. Instead, it understands everyday language and creates personalised answers from its training data (much of the internet). This helps ChatGPT deal with complicated HR questions effectively.

Though many people first use ChatGPT like Google, remember it's not for searching—it's for chatting. The quality of the output from ChatGPT is determined by the quality of your prompts. In this book, we'll explore four main types of prompts to engage with ChatGPT:

1. **Generating content:** This is the basic function where you input a prompt and receive a response.

2. **Refining responses with follow-up questions:** If the initial answer doesn't meet your needs, you can ask further questions. For instance, if a complicated molecular biology explanation is given, you can request a simpler explanation—like asking ChatGPT to explain it as if you were a 12-year-old.

   You can also modify the conversation's tone, ranging from serious to playful, based on your preferences. For instance, you might want a response in the style of Bill Clinton, or request a friendlier tone. For a more organised answer, ask ChatGPT to present the data in a table format.

   To dig deeper, request further explanation on specific points or ask for additional details. For a creative spin, you could even ask ChatGPT to turn a response into a poem or song.

3. **Reviewing, summarising, and refining existing content:** One of ChatGPT's powerful abilities is refining your content. You can paste an overly long email into the prompt and ask ChatGPT to make it clearer and more concise. This is increasingly used by companies to rewrite policies for easy understanding.

4. **Comparative analysis:** You can compare two blog articles or CVs by feeding them into ChatGPT and asking it to compare them. For example, in an HR context, you could anonymise CVs as 'Candidate 1' and 'Candidate 2', and have ChatGPT evaluate them against the job description's requirements. So, don't be afraid to experiment and discover various ways to engage with ChatGPT.

Writing clear prompts is key to getting helpful answers from ChatGPT. If you ask a specific question, you'll get a more useful and accurate answer. Remember, ChatGPT uses billions of sentences to form its responses, so the more exact your question, the better its answer will be.

ChatGPT remembers what's been said during a chat. It uses this information to make sense of new questions and past conversations.

The Interface

In the picture below, you can see the ChatGPT interface. It has features to make using the AI easy.

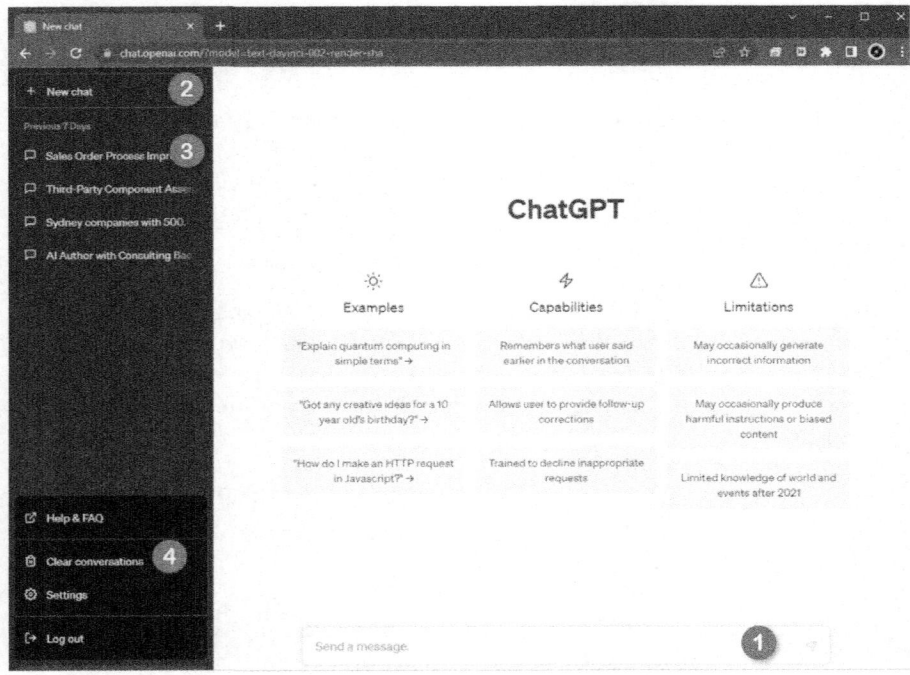

When you type a prompt (1), it starts a new chat. Your old chats are on the left (2), so you can look at them or continue them anytime. If you want to start a new chat while you're in another, just click "New Chat" (3). And if you want to get rid of old chats, use the "Clear" button.

Why save conversations with ChatGPT? Think of this: You have one chat where you're writing job descriptions and another where you're changing emails to a specific style. Saving these chats means you can use the same instructions again, saving you time. We'll show this in more detail with examples later.

When you receive an answer from ChatGPT that isn't to your liking, you don't need to rephrase your question or input again. Instead, you can simply utilise the 'Regenerate Response' button, a feature designed to prompt ChatGPT to produce an alternative response.

This button can be found in the same window where the bot's reply appears. Clicking on it initiates a process where ChatGPT reevaluates your query and offers a new, and hopefully more suitable, response.

The 'Regenerate Response' function doesn't guarantee a better answer every time. It merely provides an alternative interpretation of your input. If you find the newly generated response still unsatisfactory, you might want to rephrase your question or provide more context. This helps the model understand your request better and generate a more accurate response.

↻ Regenerate response

As you read this book, the types of prompts we've discussed will start to make sense with our examples. To understand better, open ChatGPT and try out these prompts. You'll get to experience the tool in a conversation.

This book won't cover the technical details of tailoring ChatGPT to your company's data. That's complex and needs another book entirely. Instead, we'll look at the basic, public version of ChatGPT that anyone can use.

Chapter Summary/Key Takeaways

1. ChatGPT is an advanced language model that can generate personalised, human-like responses, making it efficient and effective for handling complex queries.

2. ChatGPT is a conversational tool, not a search engine, and can perform various functions:

- Generate content with prompts
- Refine responses using follow-up questions
- Review, summarise, and refine existing content
- Conduct comparative analysis

3. Crafting precise requests ensures relevant and accurate responses from ChatGPT.

4. ChatGPT can maintain context throughout conversations, considering follow-up questions and prior interactions.

5. The ChatGPT interface allows users to start new chats, save conversations, and access previous chats easily.

6. Experimenting with different prompts and interactions helps users better understand and experience the capabilities of ChatGPT.

As you progress through the book, these concepts will become clearer through examples and hands-on experience with the ChatGPT interface.

4 BEFORE YOU GET STARTED

In this chapter you will learn:

- The importance of data privacy and security while using ChatGPT and how to reduce the risk of your data being associated with your company.

- The necessity of integrating your expertise, particularly in legal or other specialised fields, into the ChatGPT's output to ensure accuracy and applicability.

- How ChatGPT uses input data to learn and grow, and how you can influence this process while safeguarding your Intellectual Property.

- The benefits and additional features offered by subscribing to ChatGPT Plus, such as preferential access and the ability to use more advanced versions of the AI model.

Reduce the risk of your data being associated with your company.

If you have registered with your professional email address, we recommend deleting your current account and creating a new one. Be aware that this will permanently delete all your previous prompts and remove your data from the ChatGPT database.

For registration, it is advisable to use a Gmail account or another free email service. For enhanced security, consider creating a new Gmail account without using your real name. This strategy helps ensure that any data entered is not linked to your personal or professional identity.

It is crucial to use a unique and complex password for your ChatGPT account to significantly reduce the risk of hacking.

Additionally, regularly clearing your chat history is a good practice; the reasons for this will be explained in a forthcoming chapter.

Finally, refrain from entering confidential information—such as proprietary company data or personally identifiable information like individual contact details—into your prompts.

Remember, ChatGPT's outputs should be treated as initial drafts for you to review and refine. Think of it as your digital intern.

ChatGPT has been trained on extensive online data, which isn't always accurate and may reflect prevalent biases. It generates responses based on statistical likelihoods from its training data. However, as an expert, your role is to verify that ChatGPT's outputs are accurate and relevant to your context. Use these outputs as a foundation to apply your expertise and understanding of your field.

As an expert in your country's HR legislation, integrating your expertise into responses from ChatGPT is essential. You must ensure that the content generated reflects the most current and applicable laws and regulations..

Additionally, if ChatGPT cannot find an answer to your question, it will attempt to construct the most plausible response, which may be incorrect. Thus, do not rely solely on the initial outputs.

ChatGPT continually learns and updates from user interactions. OpenAI's terms disclose that your prompts could help train the model, potentially making any company IP you input accessible in other users' responses. However, you can opt out of this by adjusting your settings to prevent your prompts from being used as training data (see below how to do this).

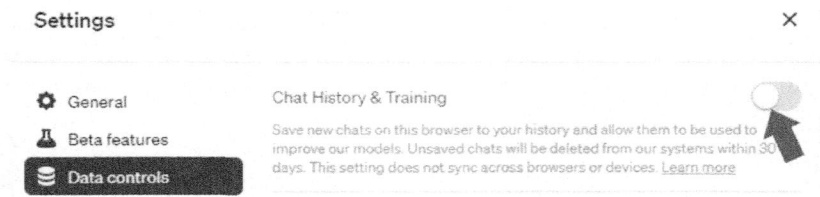

Consider signing up for ChatGPT Plus

Although not a requirement, subscribing to this service grants you access to a significantly more intelligent version of ChatGPT (you'll see a toggle button at the top of your chats to use GPT-4).

Our most capable model, great for tasks that require creativity and advanced reasoning.

Available exclusively to Plus users

ChatGPT Plus provides you with preferential access, even during times of peak user engagement; a feature early adopters might have noticed to be crucial as they might have faced restricted access during such high activity periods. Priced at 20 USD per month, a subscription to ChatGPT Plus is recommended.

Chapter Summary/Key Takeaways

1. Privacy and Security: Use an anonymous email for ChatGPT, create a complex password, clear chat history regularly, and avoid sharing sensitive information.

2. Expert Input: ChatGPT is a tool, not a final authority. Leverage your expertise to ensure output accuracy and relevance, particularly in specialised fields.

3. AI Learning: ChatGPT learns from user inputs. Protect your IP by preventing your prompts from being used as training data.

4. ChatGPT Plus Benefits: Subscribing offers enhanced AI capability and preferential access, particularly useful during peak usage times.

5 USE CASES OF CHATGPT IN HR

In this chapter, we explore the broad spectrum of activities typically managed by HR. We will demonstrate, with examples, how ChatGPT can streamline these processes, featuring relevant prompts and responses from ChatGPT.

Human Resources processes comprise activities designed to help organisations manage their employees effectively. Here are the main HR processes (with an asterisk denoting the ones that we'll demonstrate with ChatGPT use cases):

1. **Recruitment***: Identifying job openings, advertising positions, screening and interviewing candidates, and hiring the best-suited individuals for the organisation.

2. **Onboarding and orientation***: Introducing new employees to the company's culture, policies, and procedures, and providing them with the necessary tools and resources to settle into their new roles.

3. **Training and development***: Assessing employee skills and competencies, designing and implementing training programmes, and supporting employee growth through continuous learning opportunities.

4. **Performance management***: Establishing performance goals, conducting regular evaluations, providing feedback, and managing underperformance to ensure employees meet organisational objectives.

5. **Compensation and benefits**: Designing competitive salary structures, administering employee benefits, and managing payroll to ensure fair and equitable remuneration for all employees.

6. Employee relations: Maintaining a positive work environment, addressing employee concerns, and resolving conflicts to promote harmonious workplace relationships.

7. Health and safety*: Ensuring a safe working environment by implementing health and safety policies, conducting risk assessments, and providing appropriate training to prevent accidents and injuries.

8. Legal compliance: Ensuring that the organisation adheres to all relevant employment laws, regulations, and industry standards, which may include anti-discrimination, equal pay, and occupational health and safety regulations.

9. Diversity and inclusion*: Promoting a diverse and inclusive workforce by implementing policies and initiatives that support equal opportunities, respect, and collaboration among employees from different backgrounds and perspectives.

10. Talent management and succession planning: Identifying high-potential employees, providing them with development opportunities, and preparing them for leadership roles to ensure the long-term success of the organisation.

11. HR administration*: Managing employee records, leave requests, and HR-related documentation to ensure accurate and up-to-date information is maintained for all employees.

* included in the following use case examples

Use Case 1 - Recruitment

Hiring the right people involves multiple steps: defining the job role, advertising the position, tracking applicants, reviewing applications, conducting interviews, verifying backgrounds and references, and offering the job, which may include negotiations. These steps may vary depending on the company and the position. With this foundational understanding of the hiring process, let's begin incorporating ChatGPT.

1. **Defining the job role**: Create a detailed job description and specification, outlining the responsibilities, requirements, and qualifications needed for the position.

Example starting prompt: "as an HR expert, write me a job description for a financial controller"

You'll get a generic response along the lines of the below:

Job Title: Financial Controller
Overview: We are seeking an experienced Financial Controller to manage the financial operations of our organisation. The successful candidate will be responsible for managing and overseeing the financial accounting, reporting, budgeting, and forecasting processes.

Key Responsibilities:
- *Manage and oversee the company's financial accounting, monitoring and reporting systems*
- *Ensure compliance with financial regulations and reporting requirements*
- *Develop financial policies and procedures to improve efficiency and accuracy*
- *Prepare and manage budgets and financial forecasts*
- *Analyse financial data and provide strategic recommendations to senior management*
- *Manage and oversee accounts payable and accounts receivable processes*
- *Manage and oversee payroll processes*
- *Ensure timely and accurate completion of month-end and year-end closing processes*
- *Coordinate with external auditors during annual audits*
- *Ensure accurate and timely tax filings and compliance with tax regulations*

- Identify and implement process improvements to increase efficiency and reduce costs
- Provide financial support to other departments as needed

Qualifications:
- Bachelor's degree in Accounting, Finance or related field
- Certified Public Accountant (CPA) designation preferred
- Minimum of 5 years of experience in financial management or accounting roles
- Strong understanding of accounting principles and financial regulations
- Excellent analytical, problem-solving and communication skills
- Ability to manage multiple tasks and prioritise effectively
- Strong leadership and team management skills
- Proficient in financial software and Microsoft Office suite

If you have the qualifications and experience we are seeking, we encourage you to apply for this exciting opportunity as a Financial Controller.

… which is a decent start but we'd like to make it specific to our organisation so we might want to give it an example of a previous job ad and get it to rewrite the above response in a style tailored to that of your organisation. To do this, we're going to give ChatGPT a follow-up prompt.

Example follow-up prompt: *"Please rewrite the above financial controller job description in the style of the following example including the information about our company:"* (after which you can paste an example from the past for ChatGPT to use in its next response)

This may have given a pretty good result, but let's say that it was now a little too long for our liking, or once we'd tested it with a text analyser and found that it needed to be clearer.

Example refining prompt: "Now re-write the original job description to be more concise and readable" or "Now re-write this job description in fewer than 600 words and write in inclusive language"

We might go through this process twice with some different prompts and get two versions which we don't have a clear preference for. We can get ChatGPT to help us decide with an analysis prompt.

Example analysis prompt: *"I will paste two job descriptions which I'd like you to do a comparative analysis of and make a recommendation for which is better for the role of financial controller"*

2. **Job posting and advertisement**: Advertise the job opening through various channels, such as job boards, social media, recruitment agencies, and the company's website, to attract a diverse pool of candidates.

For this, we're going to use ChatGPT as a research tool to determine which channels are best for this job type.

Example starting prompt: *"Which recruitment agencies specialise in recruitment of financial roles in New York?"*

In its response, ChatGPT acknowledges that the information that it has access to might be out of date (remember, its training data is only up to January 2022 in the free version) but the answer is reasonable.

While I don't have access to real-time information or specific recommendations, I can provide you with a list of well-known recruitment agencies that often specialise in financial roles in New York. These agencies have a strong presence in the financial industry and may be worth considering:

1. Robert Half
2. Michael Page
3. Randstad
4. Hudson
5. Accountemps
6. Adecco
7. Kforce
8. Execu|Search
9. Beacon Hill Staffing Group
10. Selby Jennings

It's important to note that the effectiveness and specialisation of these agencies may vary over time, so I recommend conducting additional research to evaluate their current capabilities, client reviews, and specific expertise in the financial sector. Checking their websites and reaching out to them directly can provide you with more accurate and up-to-date information on their services and specialisation.

Additionally, networking with professionals in the financial industry, checking job boards, and utilizing online platforms such as LinkedIn can also help you identify suitable recruitment agencies in New York for financial roles.

When I did this search, the first response from ChatGPT was that it couldn't help me but when this happens you have two ways of getting a better answer: (1) by clicking on "regenerate response" it gave me the above answer which is a good part of the way there or (2) you can give the answer a thumbs down and you will be prompted to evaluate alternative responses.

Example follow-up prompt: *"Give me ten more"*

... and hey presto – I've got a pretty good list of agencies to research further.

3. **Applicant tracking:** Collect and organise applications received from candidates, often using an Applicant Tracking System (ATS) to streamline the process.

Using the example of a company who has either just started up or has grown to the size that they now require an Applicant Tracking System.

Example starting and comparative analysis prompt: *"As an HR systems expert, provide me with a list of the top ten applicant tracking systems. Please include these in a table with columns for the pros and cons of each system. My company is in the mining industry and at any one time we have between 5 and 10 jobs that we're recruiting for"*

Notice that I'm asking ChatGPT to act as an HR systems expert and telling it what our likely volume requirements are, and our industry, to give it context and to get a higher quality answer. Here's what it returns (on the following page).

ATS Name	Pros	Cons
1. Workable	- Easy to use interface - Good for smaller numbers of job postings - Wide range of integrations	- Not tailored to specific industries - Pricing can be a bit high
2. Greenhouse	- Provides strong analytics - Extensive interview and hiring process structure	- Can be complex to navigate - Pricing may be high for smaller businesses
3. Jobvite	- Great for building candidate relationships - Good at managing referrals	- The interface can be complex - Customer support may be slow
4. Bullhorn	- Designed for staffing and recruiting agencies - Excellent customer service	- Not as straightforward for direct employers - May have more features than needed
5. iCIMS	- Comprehensive solution, from recruitment to onboarding - Customizable workflows	- Not the most intuitive interface - May require technical support for setup
6. Lever	- User-friendly - Good collaborative tools	- Pricing can be high - More features than smaller businesses may need
7. SmartRecruiters	- Strong integration options - Good candidate experience	- The interface may be complex - Reporting capabilities can be limited

8. JazzHR	• Great for small to medium businesses • Good pricing plans	• Fewer integrations compared to others • Limited customisation
9. BreezyHR	• Good for candidate management and communication • User-friendly interface	• Reporting could be improved • Limited advanced features
10. Zoho Recruit	• Good integration with other Zoho products • Cost-effective for smaller businesses	• Not as feature-rich as some other options • Customer support can be slow

I'm happy with this table that I can then use to support my research and decision-making process.

4. **Screening and shortlisting:** Review the applications to identify candidates who meet the job requirements. This may involve evaluating CVs, cover letters, and application forms, as well as conducting initial phone or video interviews.

We're going to demonstrate a few different prompt types in one here as we're going to ask ChatGPT to evaluate CVs not only against each other but also in relation to the job description since it contains our key requirements.

Something to note when analysing long text is that (at the time of writing this book but that may change in future) ChatGPT has a limit on the number of characters that you can include in a prompt. For long CVs this can present a problem but not one that is insurmountable – remember that it's a conversation, not a single prompt, so you can start off by telling ChatGPT what you're going to provide in the following prompts and it will acknowledge this in its response. Sometimes it will start generating the result ahead of time (in this example, possibly after you provide the first CV) but you can click on the button to say "Stop Generating" and continue to provide the information in your prompts.

Example starting prompt: *I'm going to provide you with three candidates' CVs and a job description. I would like you to evaluate the CVs in a table with the requirements from the job description in the leftmost column and then a comment about how each CV rates against these requirements in the subsequent columns.*

Example follow-up prompt: *Reorder the table so that CVs are ranked from most suitable CV is on the left and least suitable on the* *right*

This demonstrates the immense power of ChatGPT as an analytical tool on unstructured data.

5. Interviewing: Conduct in-depth interviews with shortlisted candidates, either in person or via video calls. This stage may involve multiple rounds of interviews and could include panel interviews, behavioural or competency-based interviews, and technical or task-based assessments.

In the above example, we used the criteria from the job description to do the evaluation of the CVs. We can use this technique again but this time, we're going to use it to generate some areas to probe in our interview questioning. You can either continue the above conversation if you've saved it or you can repeat the process, this time focusing on one CV at a time.

Example starting prompt: *"I'm going to provide you with a candidate's CVs and a job description. As a recruitment expert I would like you to evaluate the CV in a table with the requirements from the job description in the leftmost column and then some questions based on the information in the CV to ask in an interview, particularly where the candidate doesn't appear to meet a requirement."*

Example follow-up prompt: *"Rewrite this table with two new columns included. One for me to enter a score and another with guidance on how to score their response to that criterion."*

Example follow-up prompt: *"Include the above in a set of questions for an interview of this candidate"*

All of which we could have done manually but using the outputs from the above prompts will save an enormous amount of time and we can refine the results with our own knowledge of our own context.

5. **Background and reference checks:** Verify the candidate's employment history, qualifications, and references to ensure the information provided is accurate and the candidate is suitable for the role.

A simple way to assist with this task is in writing communications.

Example starting prompt: *"As a recruitment expert, write me an email to a candidate's previous employer to verify their position there.*

The candidate, Michael Johnson, claims to have worked at Company XYZ from April 2015 to May 2023"

Here's the result:

Subject: Employment Verification Request - Michael Johnson

Dear [Previous Employer's Name],

I hope this message finds you well. My name is [Your Name], and I am a Recruitment Specialist at [Your Company Name]. We are currently in the process of evaluating Michael Johnson as a potential candidate for a position with our organisation.

Michael has listed Company XYZ as a previous employer, where he mentioned working from April 2015 to May 2023. In order to ensure we have accurate information about his employment history, I kindly request your assistance in verifying the following details:

1. Duration of employment: Please confirm if Michael Johnson was employed at Company XYZ from April 2015 to May 2023.
2. Position held: Can you please provide details about the position(s) held by Michael during his tenure at Company XYZ?
3. Job responsibilities: We would appreciate a brief overview of Michael's primary job responsibilities in his role(s) at Company XYZ.
4. Performance: If you are able to share, we would appreciate any insight into Michael's performance, including notable achievements, strengths, or areas for improvement.
5. Reason for leaving: Could you please inform us of the circumstances surrounding Michael's departure from Company XYZ?

Please note that we have received written consent from Michael Johnson to contact you for this information. If you require any additional information or documentation, kindly let me know and I will promptly provide the necessary materials.

We greatly appreciate your prompt assistance in this matter, as it will *help us make an informed decision regarding Michael's application. If you have any questions or concerns, please do not hesitate to reach out to me via email or phone at [Your Phone Number].*

Thank you for your time and consideration.

Sincerely,
[Your Full Name] Recruitment Specialist

… a pretty good starting point for us to tailor to our requirements.

6. **Job offer and negotiation:** Present a formal job offer to the selected candidate, including details of salary, benefits, and other terms of employment. This stage may involve negotiation to reach a mutually agreeable arrangement.

Example starting prompt: *"A candidate that we'd like to hire is requesting a higher salary than we can afford. Write me a negotiation meeting outline with some considerations of alternative value that we can offer."*

An important benefit of ChatGPT is shown in this example, which is the ability to help us to think of alternatives when we're stuck in a situation. You might have thought of all of the alternatives below but it would have taken time to do so. Here are the alternative value propositions presented to us by ChatGPT as part of the response.

Within the ChatGPT response was the following:

Alternative Value Propositions

Flexible work arrangements
- *Remote work options*
- *Flexible work hours*
- *Compressed workweeks*

Professional development opportunities
- *Tuition reimbursement*
- *Access to online courses and certifications*
- *In-house training programs*

- Conference attendance

Enhanced employee benefits
- Health and wellness benefits
- Retirement plans and contributions
- Life and disability insurance

Additional paid time off
- Additional vacation days
- Personal days
- Volunteer days

Performance-based incentives
- Bonuses tied to company or individual performance
- Stock options or equity grants
- Clearly defined promotion pathways and timelines

Some points for consideration in here which I would find useful and whilst I may have eventually come up with all of these myself, it would have taken a lot more time than ChatGPT took to derive.

7. **Other example starting prompts useful for your recruitment process:**

"Write an employment offer letter for the role of Chief Data Scientist along with an accompanying email to attach the letter to"

"Write a polite email notifying a candidate that they have been unsuccessful in their application for the role of Procurement Category Manager at our organisation"

Use Case Summary/Key Takeaways

1. Recruitment is a critical process in any organisation, and utilising AI-powered tools like ChatGPT can streamline the process and save time.

2. ChatGPT can help generate job descriptions, identify the most suitable candidates, and even develop interview questions based on the job requirements and candidate's CV.

3. When evaluating CVs, ChatGPT can create a table comparing candidates against job requirements, and even rank them from the most to the least suitable.

4. Use ChatGPT to prepare for interviews by generating questions to probe areas where a candidate might not meet the job requirements. The AI can also help you create a scoring system to assess the candidate's responses.

5. ChatGPT can assist with background and reference checks by drafting emails to verify a candidate's employment history.

6. When negotiating job offers, ChatGPT can help you brainstorm alternative value propositions if a candidate requests a higher salary than the organisation can afford.

7. The AI-powered tool can also create important documents like employment offer letters, rejection emails, and onboarding materials.

By leveraging ChatGPT's capabilities, recruiters can save time, ensure thorough evaluations, and enhance the overall recruitment process.

In the next use case, you will learn the various ways in which ChatGPT can be integrated into the onboarding process for new employees.

Use Case 2 - Onboarding

We will explore the primary goals of the onboarding process: to seamlessly integrate new staff into the company, familiarise them with the company's culture, and support their long-term success. Although approaches may vary across different organisations, we will demonstrate how ChatGPT can be instrumental in achieving these aims.

ChatGPT can support HR teams in crafting welcoming messages, producing and sharing onboarding resources like handbooks, training guides, and induction schedules. With its ability to understand and generate natural language, ChatGPT can create clear and concise content tailored to your company's needs.

Integrating ChatGPT into the onboarding process can enhance efficiency and experience for HR professionals and the new employees alike.

For instance, if your onboarding document has become too complex over time, ChatGPT can help to make it more straightforward and concise. This ensures that new staff can understand their roles, compliance requirements, and feel better equipped to perform their jobs effectively.

Some practical examples of **refining** prompts:

"I will provide you with our Equal Employment Opportunity policy – summarise this simply in three sentences for inclusion in our onboarding guidance document" (and paste your policy in here)

"I will provide you with our existing employee onboarding manual. As an HR expert, reword this to be clearer and more succinct" (and paste your existing employee onboarding manual text in here)

1. Preparing for the Arrival of the New Employee: You may have your onboarding documentation and task lists scattered around which you could include in your prompt. Let's say that in this case, we are a start-up and we don't have legacy information for inclusion in our prompt.

Example starting prompt: *"as an HR expert, provide me with an onboarding checklist for a new employee who hasn't started yet. The checklist should include what we need to do and what the employee needs to do in two sections"*

Example response from ChatGPT:

"here's a basic onboarding checklist for your new employee. Remember, this is a general list and it's always a good idea to tailor it to your specific business and the role the new hire will fill.

What We (the Employer) Need to Do:

- **Prepare Paperwork**: This includes the employment contract, tax forms, direct deposit forms, and any other necessary documents.

- **Setup Payroll**: Ensure that the new employee is added to the payroll system.

- **Create an Email Account**: Provide an email account, if applicable, for the employee.

- **Setup Hardware/Software**: Prepare any necessary equipment, such as a laptop, and ensure access to necessary software and systems.

- **Prepare Workspace**: If the employee will be working in an office, ensure their workspace is clean and stocked with necessary supplies.

- **Arrange Access**: Provide access cards, keys, or codes as necessary.

- **Prepare Training Materials**: This may include an employee handbook, training videos, or other resources.

- **Schedule Orientation**: Plan a day or more (depending on your organisation) to introduce the employee to the company, their role, and their colleagues.

- **Assign a Mentor/Buddy**: Designate a more experienced team member to help the new hire get settled in.

- **Communicate with the Team**: Let the team know when the new hire will start and what their role will be.

- **Organise First Week Schedule**: Plan meetings, training sessions, and other activities for the new hire's first week.

What the New Employee Needs to Do:

- **Review and Sign Employment Contract**: They should understand the terms and conditions of their employment.

- **Complete and Return All Necessary Paperwork**: This may include tax forms, direct deposit forms, and other documents.

- **Setup Email Account**: If provided by the employer, the new hire should ensure they can access their email account.

- **Familiarise with Hardware/Software**: They should make sure they know how to use all necessary equipment and systems.

- **Review Training Materials**: They should go through all provided materials and be prepared to ask questions about anything they don't understand.

- **Attend Orientation**: They should be present and engaged during all orientation activities.

- **Meet with Mentor/Buddy**: They should spend time with the assigned mentor to learn more about the role and the company.

- **Get to Know the Team**: They should make an effort to meet their new colleagues and learn about their roles within the team.

- **Follow First Week Schedule**: They should attend all scheduled meetings and training sessions.

Remember, onboarding is not just about the first day or week. Effective onboarding can take up to a year, and is about helping the new employee become a productive and satisfied member of your team. Check in regularly with the new employee and provide ongoing support as they learn their role and become part of the company."

As ChatGPT has advised, we'll tailor it to our company which you can either do by taking this version and giving ChatGPT follow-up prompts on what you want to change.

2. Welcome the New Employee: On the first day, HR should welcome the new employee and introduce them to their team. They should also provide a tour of the workplace (unless the role is entirely remote) and review the company policies and procedures. We will proceed with the discussion on the onboarding checklist from the previous point to illustrate how ChatGPT can adapt its response style based on the provided context.

Example follow-up prompt: *"Using the above checklist as a reference, write a welcome email to this new employee which is to be sent to them first thing on the day that they start with our company"*

Example response from ChatGPT:

"Subject: Welcome to Our Team, [Employee's Name]!

Dear [Employee's Name],

Welcome to [Company Name]! We are thrilled to have you on board and look forward to seeing the great things we know you will accomplish here.

Today is your first day, and we have quite a few things planned to get you started. We believe that a smooth start is key to a successful journey. Here's a brief rundown of what to expect:

- ***Orientation Session***: *We have scheduled an orientation session for you at [time]. This will give you an overview of our company's mission, culture, and values.*

- ***Workspace and Tools***: *We have set up your workspace and the necessary hardware and software that you will need for your role. If you encounter any issues, please reach out to our IT department at [IT Support Email/Extension].*

- ***Email and Systems Access***: *Your company email address and access to our internal systems have been set up. Your username is [Username] and temporary password is [Password]. You will be prompted to change this when you first log in.*

- **Meet your Mentor/Buddy**: [Mentor's Name], a member of your team, has been assigned as your buddy. They will be available to answer any questions you might have and will help you get acquainted with the team and our workflows.

- **First Week Schedule**: You will find your schedule for the first week attached to this email. It includes a mix of training sessions, team meetings, and one-on-one sessions with key team members.

Remember, we are here to support you. If you have any questions or need any assistance, feel free to ask. Your team lead, [Team Lead's Name], and HR representative, [HR Representative's Name], are always available to help you out.

We know that starting a new job can be daunting, but we want you to know that you are joining a team that values collaboration, mutual support, and continued learning. We have all been where you are, and we are all here to ensure your success.

We're excited to have you join us and can't wait to see what we will achieve together. Welcome to the team, [Employee's Name]!

Best Regards,

[Your Name]

[Your Position]

[Company Name]

[Your Contact Information]"

A reasonable starting point for us to edit to suit our scenario!

3. Provide Training: HR should provide the new employee with any necessary training to help them understand their job duties, the company culture, and any relevant technology or systems.

As an example, following on from the above, once the new employee has read all of the required information, we want to test their knowledge of them.

Example starting prompt: *"write a five-question multiple choice test on the following policy (give the correct answers after the test for the marker to refer to)"*

The response from ChatGPT should be checked for accuracy and then can be put directly into your company's learning management system and the process can be repeated for other documentation with which you expect your new users to be familiar.

4. Set Expectations: HR should set expectations for the new employee's performance, including job responsibilities, goals, and objectives.

Example starting prompt: *"I will provide you with a job description for a new starter. Use this to draft a message to this new employee to include their job responsibilities goals and objectives using the OKR framework for performance management"* … and paste the text of their job description and you could include their objectives and key results (OKR) but ChatGPT will have a good first go at these if you haven't created them yet.

5. Monitor Progress: HR should monitor the new employee's progress during the first few months and provide feedback to help them improve.

Example starting prompt: *"Here is all of the feedback received by an employee from an anonymous 360 degree survey. Summarise this for their upcoming performance review meeting"*

6. Follow Up: After the onboarding process, HR should follow up with the new employee to ensure that they are happy and comfortable in their new role and offer some advice.

Example starting prompt: *"What are some strategies for managing stress and maintaining work-life balance?"*

Use Case Summary/Key Takeaways

This use case discusses the various ways in which ChatGPT can be integrated into the onboarding process for new employees. It demonstrates how the AI can assist in creating welcoming communications, refining onboarding materials, and developing clear, concise content tailored to the organisation's needs. The chapter also provides practical examples of refining prompts and onboarding checklists, showing how ChatGPT can help to streamline the onboarding experience.

Key Takeaways:

1. ChatGPT can assist in developing comprehensive onboarding materials, including employee handbooks, training guides, and orientation schedules, by utilising its natural language processing capabilities.

2. The AI can create a more seamless and effective onboarding process for HR professionals and new employees alike.

3. Specific examples of refining prompts highlight how ChatGPT can succinctly summarise policies and rewrite existing onboarding manuals for clarity

4. ChatGPT can assist in preparing onboarding checklists for new employees, detailing the responsibilities of both the employer and the employee.

5. The AI can help draft welcome emails to new employees, incorporating elements of the onboarding checklist.

6. ChatGPT can be used to generate training materials, such as multiple-choice tests, based on provided policies or guidelines.

7. The AI can help HR professionals set performance expectations for new employees using the OKR (Objectives and Key Results) framework.

8. ChatGPT can summarise feedback from anonymous surveys, assisting in preparing for performance review meetings.

Overall, the integration of ChatGPT into the onboarding process can not only streamline the process but also improve the experience for both HR professionals and new employees.

Use Case 3 - Performance Management

While HR is the guardian of the performance management process, many of the activities required are performed by the line managers within the organisation. Between HR and line managers, I've outlined the tasks that form the overall process of performance management below and provided examples of how ChatGPT can assist with these.

1. Setting performance goals: HR professionals work with managers to set performance goals that align with the organisation's strategic objectives. This involves defining specific, measurable, achievable, relevant, and time-bound (SMART) goals that employees will work towards.

You could include the employee's job description in your prompt or you could simply ask for some typical goals for that type of job as in the following example ...

Example starting prompt: *"What are some examples of SMART goals for a mechanical engineer"*

Here's what ChatGPT responded with:

"Sure, here are some examples of SMART goals for a mechanical engineer:

Specific: *Complete the certification course on advanced fluid dynamics within the next six months.*

- **Measurable:** *The achievement will be marked by receiving a certification.*

- **Achievable:** *This goal is achievable with consistent study and preparation.*

- **Relevant:** *The knowledge gained will aid in better understanding and application of fluid dynamics principles in mechanical engineering projects.*

- **Time-bound:** *The goal is to be achieved within six months.*

Specific: *Improve the efficiency of the current manufacturing process by 15% over the next year.*

- **Measurable:** *The efficiency improvement can be measured quantitatively.*

- **Achievable:** With proper analysis and process improvement techniques, this goal can be achieved.

- **Relevant:** Improving efficiency directly contributes to the organisation's productivity and profitability.

- **Time-bound:** The goal has a timeline of one year.

Specific: Reduce machine downtime in the production line by 20% in the next quarter.

- **Measurable:** Machine downtime can be tracked and measured.

- **Achievable:** With proper maintenance scheduling and problem-solving techniques, this goal is achievable.

- **Relevant:** Reducing downtime can increase overall productivity and efficiency.

- **Time-bound:** The goal is to be achieved by the end of the next quarter.

Specific: Design, prototype, and test a new mechanical component to replace the current failing part within three months.

- **Measurable:** The completion of the design, prototype, and testing stages will determine the achievement of this goal.

- **Achievable:** With the right skills and resources, this goal is realistic.

- **Relevant:** This task is crucial to address the problem of the failing component and ensure product quality.

- **Time-bound:** The goal is to be achieved within three months.

Specific: Publish a research paper on the innovative application of nanotechnology in mechanical engineering by the end of this year.

- **Measurable:** The publication of the paper will mark the achievement of this goal.

- **Achievable:** *With thorough research and dedication, this goal can be reached.*

- **Relevant:** *Publishing research contributes to the engineer's professional development and adds value to the mechanical engineering field.*

- **Time-bound:** *The goal is to be achieved by the end of the year."*

If these weren't aligned to what you were planning you can keep asking ChatGPT for "five more" and see what it comes back with and you'll likely get some good ideas. This method mirrors the strategies employed by numerous marketers. They often use it to create a long list of headlines for blog articles. They continue to request more iterations until they receive a result that meets their satisfaction.

You could also provide existing goals to ask whether they are SMART and get ChatGPT to update them if they are found to be deficient.

2. Development planning: After the performance review, HR professionals work with managers to identify development opportunities for employees. This may involve creating a development plan that outlines specific activities, such as training or mentoring, that will help the employee improve their performance.

Since React Native programming is a hot skill right now, let's use it in our example of getting ChatGPT to assist in this development planning process.

Example starting prompt: *"as a learning and development expert, write me a development plan for a junior react native developer who would like to progress to a leadership position within the next 5 years"*

ChatGPT does a remarkable job of plotting out the course for this junior developer and while it occasionally veers off-course from what I would consider a standard plan, the points which I wouldn't have considered if I was concocting this plan myself are good thought prompters for my own development.

Sure, I'll be happy to help you craft a development plan for your junior React Native developer. Please note that while this plan specifically targets their technical skills, it also includes broader leadership skills necessary for their career progression.

Development Plan for a Junior React Native Developer aiming for Leadership

Year 1: Strengthening Core Skills

Technical Skills: Focus on mastering React Native and JavaScript. This should include understanding the nuances of JavaScript, ES6+ features, React principles, Redux for state management, and various React Native libraries.

Project Management: Start gaining experience in project management by taking the lead on small projects or components of larger projects.

Communication Skills: Attend workshops and seminars on effective communication. Regularly practice presenting your work to peers and supervisors.

Mentorship: Request a mentor within the organisation who is in a leadership role. This person can guide you through technical challenges and provide advice on career progression.

Year 2: Broadening Technical Knowledge

Cross-Platform Knowledge: Learn about other mobile development platforms like Flutter or Swift, to broaden understanding and be able to make informed decisions in cross-platform scenarios.

Backend Understanding: Improve understanding of back-end technologies. This could be Node.js, Python, or Java depending on what is commonly used in your organisation.

Code Review: Actively participate in code reviews, both as a reviewer and reviewee. This will improve your code quality and also build your skills in giving and receiving constructive feedback.

Leadership Training: Begin attending leadership training seminars, reading relevant books, or taking online courses to better understand what effective leadership looks like.

Year 3: Deepening Expertise and Growing Influence

Advanced React & React Native: Dive into advanced topics like performance tuning, native modules, animations, and more.

DevOps: Learn about CI/CD practices, testing, and how to work with systems like Jenkins, Travis, or GitHub Actions.

People Management: Take on more responsibility in projects, including managing other developers or interns. This will provide experience in people management and delegation.

Public Speaking: Aim to present at internal meetings or external conferences. This will build your confidence and reputation within the industry.

Year 4: Fostering Innovation and Leading Projects

Innovation: Start exploring and experimenting with the latest tech trends, such as AI, machine learning, AR/VR, and how they can be integrated into mobile app development.

Project Leadership: Take the lead on significant projects within the company, showing your technical and leadership skills.

Conflict Resolution: Attend training sessions or workshops on conflict resolution, an important skill for any leader.

Networking: Network extensively both within and outside the organisation. Building relationships is crucial for a leadership role.

Year 5: Preparing for Leadership

Strategic Thinking: Start participating in strategic decision-making processes and understand the business side of projects.

Mentoring: Start mentoring junior developers. This will not only help them but also further develop your leadership and teaching skills.

Leadership Role: Express your interest in a leadership role to your superiors. Discuss with them your achievements and why you believe you're ready to take the next step.

Continue Learning: Even as you prepare to move into leadership, never stop learning. Keep yourself updated with the latest in tech, leadership, and your industry.

Remember that everyone's journey is different, and it's okay to move faster or slower through this plan. The most important thing is to keep learning and growing, both as a developer and a leader. Good luck!

A remarkable starting point for me to work with as this employee's line manager. To manage their performance in relation to this plan, I'm going to ask ChatGPT to turn it into a format more suited to evaluation.

Example starting prompt: *"write the above plan in table form for evaluation of the employee at the end of year one"*

Evaluation Criteria	Expectations	Notes
Technical Skills	Mastering React Native and JavaScript, including understanding the nuances of JavaScript, ES6+ features, React principles, Redux for state management, and various React Native libraries.	Development and mastery of technical skills is a primary focus for the first year.

Evaluation Criteria	Expectations	Notes
Project Management	Begin to gain experience in project management by taking the lead on small projects or components of larger projects.	This is an opportunity to apply technical skills in a real-world context, and to begin developing leadership skills.
Communication Skills	Attendance at workshops and seminars on effective communication. Regular practice of presenting work to peers and supervisors.	Communication is key for effective teamwork and leadership. The ability to articulate ideas clearly and persuasively will be assessed.
Mentorship	Request and engage with a mentor within the organisation who is in a leadership role, receiving guidance on technical challenges and advice on career progression.	Engagement with mentorship shows initiative and a commitment to learning. The quality of the relationship with the mentor and the ability to act on their advice will be considered.

3. Performance improvement: If an employee's performance is below expectations, HR professionals and managers work together to develop a performance improvement plan. This plan outlines specific actions that the employee can take to improve their performance, as well as a timeline for improvement.

We're going to continue with the example React Native programmer from above.

Example starting prompt: *"write me a performance improvement plan for a React Native developer. These were their goals which they are not achieving any of to a satisfactory level but we believe that they have* *potential to improve" [Paste the table from point 4 above]*

Performance Improvement Plan

Employee Name: [Employee's Name]

Position: React Native Developer

Date: [Current Date]

Review Period: [e.g. Next 3 months]

This Performance Improvement Plan (PIP) outlines specific areas where performance expectations are not being met to a satisfactory level. A plan of action is included to assist [Employee's Name] in achieving the desired performance level.

Area 1: Technical Skills

Expectation: Mastery of React Native and JavaScript, including understanding the nuances of JavaScript, ES6+ features, React principles, Redux for state management, and various React Native libraries.

Performance Gap:

[Provide specific examples of where the employee has demonstrated a lack of mastery in technical skills]

Plan of Action:

1. Attend refresher courses on React Native, JavaScript, and Redux. Set a target to complete these courses within one month.
2. Implement what has been learned in these courses in day-to-day tasks and projects.
3. Schedule bi-weekly check-ins with a senior developer to review progress, discuss challenges, and seek advice on overcoming those challenges.

Area 2: Project Management

Expectation: Begin to gain experience in project management by taking the lead on small projects or components of larger projects.

Performance Gap:

[Provide specific examples of where the employee has struggled with project management]

Plan of Action:

1. Enrol in an introductory project management course. Aim to complete this course within two months.
2. Upon completion of the course, take the lead on a small project or a component of a larger project under the supervision of a project manager.
3. Schedule regular meetings with the supervising project manager to discuss progress, identify areas for improvement, and develop strategies to address these areas.

Area 3: Communication Skills

Expectation: Attendance at workshops and seminars on effective communication. Regular practice of presenting work to peers and supervisors.

Performance Gap:

[Provide specific examples of where the employee's communication skills have been inadequate]

Plan of Action:

1. Attend a communication workshop or seminar within the next month.
2. Practice presenting work to peers and supervisors at least twice a month. Solicit feedback on presentation skills and use this feedback to improve.

3. Incorporate feedback received during presentations into future communication, demonstrating progress in this area.

Area 4: Mentorship

Expectation: Request and engage with a mentor within the organisation who is in a leadership role, receiving guidance on technical challenges and advice on career progression.

Performance Gap:

[Provide specific examples of where the employee has not effectively engaged with a mentor]

Plan of Action:

1. Identify a suitable mentor within the organisation and initiate a mentorship relationship within the next month.

2. Meet with the mentor bi-weekly to discuss technical challenges, seek advice on career progression, and receive feedback on performance.

3. Implement the advice and feedback received from the mentor in day-to-day tasks and career progression strategies.

Follow-up and Review

A formal review of this Performance Improvement Plan will take place after three months. However, progress will be assessed continuously during regular check-ins and meetings. Please note that failure to meet the expectations outlined in this plan could result in further disciplinary action.

Employee Acknowledgement

I have read and understand this Performance Improvement Plan.

Employee Signature: _____

Date: _____

Manager Signature: _____

Date: _____

You can see from this response that ChatGPT has understood the context and used its knowledge of what should go into a performance improvement plan.

4. Ongoing performance feedback: HR professionals and managers provide ongoing feedback to employees throughout the performance management cycle. This feedback should be frequent, specific, and focused on areas where the employee can improve their performance.

For this part of the performance review process, we're going to use ChatGPT to refine our email communications. The line manager of the employee has sent the draft of an email that he was planning to send to this employee which we may agree with the intention, we don't agree with the abrupt tone. Below is the original email:

Here's the **example refining prompt:** *"Below is an email to an employee about their performance. Please reword it to be clearer, more professional and polite:*

Subject: Unacceptable Performance

[Employee's Name],

Your performance has been a consistent disappointment. Despite previous warnings, you continue to fall short of the required standards. This is unacceptable and cannot be tolerated any longer.

Your lack of commitment and subpar work are not only hindering our team's progress but also reflecting poorly on the entire organisation. Immediate improvement is mandatory if you wish to remain employed here.

Consider this email a final warning. Failure to meet the required levels will result in severe consequences, including termination.

You are expected to submit a written plan outlining your strategy for improvement within 24 hours. Any further negligence will be met with swift action.

This is a wake-up call. Take it seriously and make the necessary changes."

This is an example of how ChatGPT can refine existing text while maintaining the points made within it. Wondering how that turned out? Here's ChatGPT's response:

"Subject: Required Performance Improvement

Dear [Employee's Name],

We trust this message finds you well. We need to address an ongoing concern regarding your work performance, which has unfortunately not met the company's expected standards.

Your commitment and quality work are vital for our team's success. Therefore, we urge you to improve your performance, as failure to do so could lead to further ramifications, including possible termination.

Please regard this email as a formal reminder of this necessity. To assist us, please provide a brief written plan outlining your strategies for improvement within the next 24 hours.

We appreciate your immediate attention to this matter and look forward to your positive response and improved performance.

Best regards,"

It's the same message but, just as we requested, the refined version is professional and more polite. It's important to review it with your own knowledge of local legislation to ensure that your communications are compliant.

5. Performance review: At the end of a defined period (usually annually), HR professionals and managers conduct a formal performance review with employees. This involves reviewing the employee's performance against the goals that were set, providing feedback, and rating their overall performance.

Following on from our mechanical engineer example earlier in this chapter, I'm going to use the goals provided in the next prompt.

Example starting prompt: *"My employee has the following goals. Put these into a table and give me a column with guidance for evaluation and a scoring mechanism"*

+ [paste goals here]

… and heres' what ChatGPT came back with – again, not perfect but a great starting point for further refinement by our team.

"Sure, here's a table with the goals you've asked for, along with evaluation guidance and a scoring mechanism:

Goal	Evaluation Guidance	Scoring Mechanism
Complete the certification course on advanced fluid dynamics within the next six months.	Track the progress of the course and the completion of modules. Check if the certification is received by the deadline.	Score 1 point for each module completed. 5 bonus points for achieving certification.
Improve the efficiency of the current manufacturing process by 15% over the next year.	Regularly monitor the manufacturing process to see if efficiency is improving. Measure the total efficiency gain at the end of the year.	Score 1 point for each 1% efficiency improvement, up to 15 points.
Reduce machine downtime in the production line by 20% in the next quarter.	Monitor machine downtime weekly to measure improvement. Calculate the total downtime reduction at the end of the quarter.	Score 1 point for each 1% reduction in downtime, up to 20 points.
Design, prototype, and test a new mechanical component to replace the current failing part within three months.	Review the design, prototype, and testing stages to ensure each is completed on time. Assess the functionality	Score 5 points for completing the design, 5 points for a successful prototype, and 5 points for successful testing.

	of the new component.	
Publish a research paper on the innovative application of nanotechnology in mechanical engineering by the end of this year.	Monitor the progress of the research and writing of the paper. Confirm the paper's publication by the end of the year.	Score 5 points for completing the research, 5 points for writing the paper, and 5 points for successful publication.

The scoring mechanism is based on a point system. Each goal can yield a total of 15 points, so an engineer who achieves all goals perfectly would earn a score of 75 points. Of course, this is just an example, and you can modify the scoring mechanism to fit your needs.

6. Recognition and rewards: HR professionals may work with managers to develop recognition and rewards programmes to incentivise high-performing employees and reinforce positive behaviours.

We're going to use this to create a starting point which we can then refine for our own organisation.

Example starting prompt: *"As an HR expert, provide an outline of a recognition and rewards programme to incentivise high-performing employees and reinforce positive behaviours"*

Sure, I'd be happy to help you create an outline for a recognition and rewards program. Here's a general outline to consider:

- A. **Program Purpose**
    - *Define the purpose and objectives of the program: What behaviors or results are you trying to incentivise or recognise?*
- B. **Eligibility Criteria**
    - *Clearly define who is eligible for the program and why.*

C. **Performance Metrics**

- Identify key performance indicators (KPIs) that will be used to evaluate employees for rewards and recognition. These could be based on individual or team performances.

D. **Recognition Categories**

- Identify different categories for recognition. This can include areas such as teamwork, customer service, innovation, leadership, etc.

E. **Reward Types**

- Define the types of rewards to be given. These could range from verbal recognition, certificates, trophies, monetary rewards, additional leave days, training opportunities, promotions, etc. Ensure the rewards are meaningful and desirable to the employees.

F. **Nomination and Selection Process**

- Set clear guidelines for how employees can be nominated and how winners are selected. This can be a combination of peer nominations, supervisor nominations, or based on meeting certain KPIs.

G. **Frequency of Recognition**

- Define how often the rewards and recognition will be given – monthly, quarterly, annually, or based on project completions.

H. **Communication and Publicity**

- Decide how the program will be communicated to the employees and how the winners will be announced. This could be through email announcements, newsletters, team meetings, company-wide events, etc.

I. **Program Evaluation**

- Plan for regular review and evaluation of the program to ensure it's effectively motivating employees and

> *reinforcing the desired behaviors. This can involve gathering feedback from employees, looking at changes in performance metrics, etc.*

J. **Budget**

> - *Establish a budget for the program. This should include the cost of the rewards themselves, as well as any administrative costs associated with running the program.*

Compared to starting with a blank piece of paper and potentially a large number of searches online for examples, this provides us with a structured programme which we can flesh out with our own information.

Use Case Summary/Key Takeaways

1. ChatGPT aids in crafting goals for specific job roles, supporting HR and line managers in performance management.

2. It refines communication, particularly in delivering feedback, ensuring it is clearer and more polite, as shown in the email rewording example.

3. ChatGPT assists in performance reviews by constructing tables with goals, evaluation guides, and scoring methods.

4. It helps in devising career development plans, exemplified in the plan for a junior React Native developer aiming for leadership.

5. ChatGPT is capable of formulating performance improvement plans for those struggling to meet goals, giving clear steps and timelines for progress.

6. Lastly, it can help design recognition and reward schemes to motivate high-performing employees.

In summary, ChatGPT can be a versatile tool in performance management, augmenting the process from goal-setting to rewards. While it doesn't replace human expertise, it serves as a valuable starting point for further refinement.

Use Case 4 - Learning and Development

In an organisation, the HR department plays a crucial role in learning and development, responsible for planning and managing programmes that enhance employees' skills and knowledge. This contributes to personal growth and the success of the organisation. HR's role in fostering a culture of continuous learning boosts productivity, encourages talent retention, and ensures that employees have the necessary skills to fulfil the company's strategic objectives. The significance of learning and development (L&D) is substantial as it helps attract and retain top talent, bolstering the company's competitive edge and aiding in the achievement of strategic goals.

ChatGPT can be an instrumental tool in assisting HR to meet an organisation's L&D objectives, offering opportunities for personalised learning experiences, streamlining processes, and providing valuable insights into training programme efficacy.

1. Needs assessment: Analyse the organisation's current and future needs to identify skill gaps and areas for improvement. This involves conducting surveys, interviews, focus groups, and analysing performance data.

Let's say in this case that we are starting from scratch with our L&D programme.

Example starting prompt: *"As an HR expert, write a plan to identify skill gaps and areas for improvement across our organisation. Include timeframes for each element of the plan which should span over 6 weeks"*

Certainly, here is a simple six-week plan to identify skill gaps and areas for improvement in your organisation.

Week 1: Preparation and Planning

Start by defining the key skills and competencies necessary for each role within your organisation. This will provide a clear reference point for identifying any gaps.

Week 2: Employee Self-Assessment

Distribute self-assessment forms to employees, allowing them to evaluate their own skill sets against the defined competencies for their role. Encourage them to be honest about areas they feel they could improve.

Week 3: Supervisor Assessment

Ask supervisors to review their direct reports' self-assessments and add their own insights. This step should help to provide a balanced view of where skill gaps exist.

Week 4: Analysis and Identification of Skill Gaps

Collate and analyse all the assessments to identify common skill gaps and individual areas for improvement. This process should provide a comprehensive picture of the organisation's current skill status.

Week 5: Strategy Development

Develop a strategy for addressing the identified skill gaps. This could include creating or sourcing relevant training programs, considering new hires to fill specific skill gaps, or considering ways to better utilise existing talents within the organisation.

Week 6: Feedback and Implementation

Provide feedback to employees and supervisors about the identified skill gaps and share the strategies for addressing them. Begin implementing the chosen strategies, such as enrolling employees in relevant training programs.

This plan is a starting point, and the exact timeframes may need to be adjusted depending on the size and complexity of your organisation. Remember to keep communication open throughout the process and encourage feedback from all involved.

We may tweak this to suit, and then use ChatGPT to achieve each of the objectives. For example, we could give it a list of job titles within our organisation and ask for suggestions for a list of skills for each.

2. Set objectives: Establish clear and measurable goals for the L&D programme, aligned with the organisation's strategy and objectives. Ensure that these goals address identified skill gaps and employee development needs.

Example starting prompt: *"I will provide you with our L&D programme. As an HR expert, provide suggestions for goals and objectives for each of the elements of our plan"*

Example follow-up prompt: *"I will provide you with a summary of our organisation's strategy. Rewrite the above goals and objectives and align them to those of our organisation"*

Example refining prompt: *"Now put these into a table for us to use to track our success in the achievement of our goals"*

3. Design the learning programme: Develop the structure, content, and delivery methods for the learning programme. This can include a combination of instructor-led training, e-learning, workshops, coaching, and mentoring.

We're going to use ChatGPT as a research tool in this case. Bear in mind that at the time of writing this book, ChatGPT's knowledge is only up until January 2022 (in the free version) so you will need to validate its responses and research more up-to-date courses for particular roles in your organisation (you can use Google's Bard product for this which isn't as proficient as ChatGPT for general purpose queries but for research on current topics it's a handy supplementary tool).

For the example below, we will bring this down to a departmental level, finance in this case.

Example starting prompt: *"As a learning and development expert, develop a learning programme for the following roles in our organisation including suggestions on relevant courses to the Accounting profession in the United Kingdom. Junior Accountant, Senior Accountant, Financial Analyst, Financial Controller. We are a public sector organisation"*

ChatGPT Response:

Sure, here is a proposed learning programme for each of the roles in your organisation. This plan includes both foundational and role-specific knowledge, along with soft skills that are important in the modern workplace.

Junior Accountant:

Foundational:

    i.   *Basic Accounting Principles and Standards: A course on the basics of accounting to reinforce foundational knowledge.*

ii. UK GAAP (Generally Accepted Accounting Principles): This will allow them to understand the accepted standards of accounting in the UK.

Role-Specific:

i. Introduction to Taxation in the UK: Understanding of taxation is crucial for an accountant.

ii. Excel for Accountants: Most accounting tasks require good Excel skills, so an advanced Excel course would be beneficial.

iii. Introduction to Payroll Management: Basic understanding of payroll management.

Soft Skills:

i. Communication Skills: Crucial for clear and effective communication within the team and with clients.

ii. Time Management: Helpful in managing workload effectively.

Senior Accountant:

Foundational:

i. Advanced Accounting Principles and Standards: A deeper understanding of accounting principles is important for senior accountants.

ii. IFRS (International Financial Reporting Standards): Senior accountants need to understand and be able to apply IFRS in their work.

Role-Specific:

i. Advanced Taxation in the UK: A more detailed understanding of taxation is necessary for a senior accountant.

ii. Financial Reporting and Analysis: This course would be useful in enhancing their reporting skills.

iii. Auditing and Assurance Services: Auditing is a critical task performed by senior accountants.

Soft Skills:

i. *Leadership Skills: As they may lead a team, leadership training will be beneficial.*

ii. *Critical Thinking: A course on this will help them make better decisions and solve problems more effectively.*

Financial Analyst:

Foundational:

i. *Corporate Finance: This course will help them understand the financial aspects of corporations.*

ii. *Financial Modeling: An important skill for financial analysts.*

Role-Specific:

i. *Advanced Excel and VBA: Essential for data analysis and automation of repetitive tasks.*

ii. *Financial Statement Analysis: Understanding financial statements in detail is crucial for a financial analyst.*

iii. *Risk Management: They should understand how to identify and manage financial risk.*

Soft Skills:

i. *Presentation Skills: As they often have to present their findings, a course on presentation skills would be beneficial.*

ii. *Negotiation Skills: This will help them to negotiate better deals and terms.*

I've only included the first three here to show that the language model that sits behind ChatGPT understands the nuances between different roles in a typical organisation, despite the fact that they are all within the finance function

4. Select or develop learning materials: Choose or create relevant learning resources, such as manuals, videos, presentations, or interactive tools, to support the learning objectives.

We could research the courses relevant to the training plan suggested above but, in some cases, we might want to develop course content. Let's do both here...

Example starting prompt: *"I will provide you with our sales process document which details the steps for our sales team from recording a new prospect in our system as an opportunity, to updating notes, to turning the opportunity into a quote and finally with the steps to update the quote to a sale within the system (Hubspot). As a learning and development expert, develop the outline of a course to train sales people in the process"* [paste your sales process here]

Example response:

Training Course Outline: Sales Process Mastery

Course Overview:

Introduction to the sales process and its importance in achieving sales success.

Overview of HubSpot as a powerful tool for managing the sales process effectively.

Practical exercises, case studies, and role-plays to reinforce learning.

Module 1: Prospecting

Understanding the role of prospecting in the sales process.

Identifying target customers and creating a customer profile.

Exploring various prospecting channels and techniques.

Leveraging HubSpot's prospecting tools for lead generation and management.

Practical exercises: Identifying potential leads, qualifying leads, and tracking interactions in HubSpot.

Module 2: Opportunity Management

Defining the key elements of an opportunity in the sales cycle.

Gathering and analysing prospect information to qualify opportunities.

Effectively managing and tracking opportunities using HubSpot's CRM functionality.

Collaboration and task assignment for opportunity progression.

Practical exercises: Creating and managing opportunities in HubSpot, tracking interactions, and setting reminders.

Module 3: Quote Generation

Understanding the importance of customised quotes and proposals.

Crafting persuasive and value-focused quotes using HubSpot's tools.

Incorporating pricing, terms, and conditions in the quote.

Personalisation and branding elements for impactful quotes.

Practical exercises: Creating customised quotes in HubSpot, incorporating pricing details, and personalisation.

Module 4: Sales Closure

Effective communication and presentation skills for closing sales.

Techniques for addressing prospect concerns and objections.

Negotiation strategies and tactics.

Leveraging HubSpot's deal tracking features for sales closure.

Practical exercises: Role-plays for presenting quotes, handling objections, and negotiating terms.

Module 5: Sale Handoff

Importance of seamless handoff for customer satisfaction.

Communication and coordination with internal teams.

Leveraging HubSpot's automation and integration capabilities for smooth handoff.

Documentation and information sharing for successful implementation.

Practical exercises: Role-plays for facilitating the sale handoff process using HubSpot.

Module 6: Sales Process Optimisation

Continuously improving and refining the sales process.

Analyzing sales data and metrics for insights and optimisation.

Leveraging HubSpot's reporting and analytics tools for process evaluation.

Identifying areas for improvement and implementing changes.

Practical exercises: Analyzing sales data in HubSpot, identifying areas for improvement, and implementing changes.

Course Conclusion:

Recap of key concepts and strategies learned throughout the course.

Action plan for applying the sales process effectively using HubSpot.

Resources for further learning and development.

Q&A session to address any remaining questions or concerns.

Note: The training course can be delivered in various formats, such as instructor-led sessions, workshops, online modules, or a combination of these, based on the specific requirements and preferences of the organisation and sales team.

Another good starting point for us to add the detail of. You could then get into more detail and ask

Example follow-on prompt: *Develop training content for our sales team. The course should take 1 hour to deliver and is on the Quote Generation module as outlined above.*

To which ChatGPT will provide more detail on that module along with timings for the delivery of each part that it has provided.

As in the example in the Employee Onboarding section of this book, you can use sales training content in your next prompt and ask ChatGPT to develop a multiple choice test which can be put directly into your company's learning management system.

5. Implement the programme: Launch the L&D programme, ensuring that employees have the necessary resources and support to participate effectively.

This includes scheduling training sessions, assigning trainers or facilitators, and monitoring participation.

A critical driver of success of any new or updated programme will be in the communication of it. Let's say in this case

Example starting prompt: *"As a communications expert, draft an email to all employees for the following learning and development programme and include that we will be hosting a lunchtime session online to answer employees' questions about the programme." + [paste your plan here]*

ChatGPT response:

Subject: Join Our Learning and Development Programme for Professional Growth

Dear [Company Name] Team,

We are thrilled to announce our Learning and Development Programme designed to enhance your professional skills and propel your career forward. We believe in the power of continuous learning and are committed to providing you with the necessary resources to excel in your roles.

The programme is tailored to meet the specific needs of different positions within our organisation. Here's a summary of the courses available for each role:

Junior Accountant:

- Basic Accounting Principles and Standards
- UK GAAP (Generally Accepted Accounting Principles)
- Introduction to Taxation in the UK
- Excel for Accountants
- Introduction to Payroll Management
- Soft Skills: Communication and Time Management

Senior Accountant:

- Advanced Accounting Principles and Standards

- IFRS (International Financial Reporting Standards)
- Advanced Taxation in the UK
- Financial Reporting and Analysis
- Auditing and Assurance Services
- Soft Skills: Leadership and Critical Thinking

Financial Analyst:

- Corporate Finance
- Financial Modeling
- Advanced Excel and VBA
- Financial Statement Analysis
- Risk Management
- Soft Skills: Presentation and Negotiation

To address any queries you may have regarding the programme, we will be hosting an online lunchtime session dedicated to answering your questions. Join us on [date] from [time] to [time]. This is an excellent opportunity to gain clarity and learn more about the programme.

Your professional growth is vital to us, and we encourage you to take advantage of these valuable learning opportunities. For further assistance, please reach out to the Learning and Development team at [contact details].

Thank you for your commitment to personal and professional development. Let's embark on this exciting journey together!

Best regards,

[Your Name] [Your Title/Position] [Company Name]

6. Evaluate the effectiveness: Continuously assess the effectiveness of the L&D programme by gathering feedback from participants and measuring performance improvements. This can be done through surveys, quizzes, or tests, as well as observing changes in employee behaviour and productivity.

Example starting prompt: *"As a learning and development expert, design a questionnaire that we can distribute to employees to evaluate the effectiveness of our L&D programme. Include multiple choice answers with a scoring mechanism on a scale of 1 to 5"*

ChatGPT response:

Sure, I'm happy to help with that! Here's a sample questionnaire that can be used to evaluate the effectiveness of your learning and development (L&D) programme:

Learning & Development Programme Effectiveness Questionnaire

In this survey, we will be asking you to evaluate your experience with our company's L&D programme. Your honest feedback will help us improve our L&D initiatives. For each question, please select a number from 1 to 5 where:

- *1 means "Strongly Disagree"*
- *2 means "Disagree"*
- *3 means "Neutral"*
- *4 means "Agree"*
- *5 means "Strongly Agree"*

Programme Content & Delivery

1. *The L&D programme content is relevant to my job. 1 2 3 4 5*
2. *The training materials (manuals, handouts, etc.) are of high quality. 1 2 3 4 5*
3. *The instructors demonstrate thorough knowledge of the subject matter. 1 2 3 4 5*
4. *The L&D activities are interactive and engaging. 1 2 3 4 5*

Skill Acquisition & Application

5. The programme has improved my skills in the areas covered. 1 2 3 4 5

6. I can apply the knowledge and skills gained from the programme to my work. 1 2 3 4 5

7. The programme has helped me improve my work performance. 1 2 3 4 5

Programme Organisation & Support

8. The L&D programme is well-organised (e.g., clear objectives, timely communication). 1 2 3 4 5

9. There is sufficient support available during and after the training (e.g., trainers, resources). 1 2 3 4 5

Programme Impact & Improvement

10. The L&D programme is making a positive impact on the company's performance. 1 2 3 4 5

11. I am satisfied with the current L&D programme. 1 2 3 4 5

12. I would recommend this L&D programme to a colleague. 1 2 3 4 5

Additional Comments

Please share any other comments or suggestions you have about our L&D programme:

[Open text box]

These questions provide a balance of assessing the content, delivery, applicability, organisation, and overall impact of the programme. The answers will provide your team with a general indication of how well the programme is working and where improvements might be needed.

7. Review and update the programme: Analyse the evaluation data and make adjustments to the L&D programme as needed. This may involve updating learning materials, modifying the programme's structure, or addressing any other areas of concern.

Something that we haven't done much of until now in this book is to use ChatGPT to analyse data. Let's say we've run the survey and have a table of all of the responses as follows:

Question	1 (Strongly Disagree)	2 (Disagree)	3 (Neutral)	4 (Agree)	5 (Strongly Agree)
Q1	5	10	10	25	50
Q2	2	8	15	25	50
Q3	3	10	20	27	40
Q4	4	12	15	29	40
Q5	20	30	20	15	15
Q6	25	25	15	20	15
Q7	15	35	20	20	10
Q8	5	10	20	30	35
Q9	3	10	15	35	37
Q10	7	8	15	35	35
Q11	5	10	20	35	30

We're going to get ChatGPT to analyse the data for us and provide insights.

Example starting prompt: *"In separate prompts I will provide you with the survey questions and then a table of responses. I want you to analyse the results and provide some insights as to the effectiveness of our L&D programme and suggestions of where and how we could improve"*

You can then paste in the next two prompts provide the original test and the table of results. Don't worry that the table doesn't retain its table format when you paste it in, ChatGPT does a great job of reconstructing the table in its analysis.

Here's the analysis that ChatGPT gave us in response to the results:

Based on the data from the summary table, let's analyse the results.

General Analysis

Generally, there is a strong positivity towards the L&D programme, particularly in areas such as content relevance (Q1), quality of materials (Q2), and support availability (Q9). The instructors' subject knowledge (Q3) and programme organisation (Q8) also received fairly positive feedback.

Specific Insights

Skill Acquisition & Application: Questions 5, 6, and 7 have the lowest average scores. The scores suggest that although the programme is well-received in terms of its content and delivery, it might not be as effective in fostering skill development and application to work. There seems to be a gap between knowledge acquisition and practical implementation.

Programme Impact: Responses to Q10 suggest that not all employees see a clear connection between the L&D programme and its impact on the company's performance. It may be worthwhile to communicate this impact more explicitly or review how it's being measured.

Suggestions for Improvement

Skill Application: For Skill Acquisition & Application, consider adding more hands-on, experiential learning components or simulations where employees can practice new skills in a controlled setting. Also, ensure that there is follow-up or "booster" sessions to reinforce learning and encourage application on the job.

Mentorship or Coaching: Incorporate a mentorship or coaching system where employees can seek advice on how to apply new skills or deal with specific challenges in their roles. This could also provide a platform for peer learning.

Feedback Loop: Implement a regular feedback loop where employees can express their challenges in applying learned skills. Use this feedback to continually refine the L&D programme.

Communicating Impact: Provide clear and regular updates on how the L&D initiatives are making a positive difference in the company's performance. Showcase specific examples or case studies where skills learned in the programme led to improvements in efficiency, problem-solving, or innovation.

It's important to carefully analyse your survey results and potentially follow up with more detailed questions or interviews to fully understand employee experiences and needs.

Again, nothing we couldn't have done manually but this will get us 90% of the way to completing the analysis.

7. Continuous improvement: Establish a culture of continuous learning and development by encouraging employees to actively seek opportunities for growth and improvement. This can include offering ongoing professional development opportunities, creating mentorship programmes, and supporting a learning-oriented work environment.

Example starting prompt: *"As an HR expert, tell me how I can go about implementing a mentorship programme in my company."*

ChatGPT Response:

Implementing a mentorship program in your company is a great way to boost employee development, foster a positive company culture, and improve overall performance. As a large multinational advertising company, you likely have a diverse workforce with a wealth of skills and experiences that can be shared. Here's a step-by-step guide on how to create an effective mentorship program:

Identify the Objectives of the Program:

The first step to creating a mentorship program is to clearly define its objectives. Are you aiming to improve employee skill sets? Do you want to help new hires acclimate to the company culture? Are you trying to increase employee retention? Once you've established your goals, you can structure the program accordingly.

Get Top-Level Buy-In:

You'll need support from executives and managers to successfully implement a mentorship program. Make sure to communicate the benefits and the value of mentorship for the organisation such as enhancing staff skills, retaining key talent, and fostering a positive corporate culture.

Define the Structure of the Program:

There are different structures you can choose for a mentorship program. This includes one-on-one mentorship, group mentorship, or a combination of both. You could also have a formal structure where mentors and mentees follow a set curriculum, or it could be informal where the pairs decide their direction. The best structure will depend on the needs of your organisation and the resources available.

Establish Criteria for Mentors and Mentees:

You'll need to decide who can be a mentor and who can be a mentee. For mentors, you may want to select experienced employees with a history of successful performance and good communication skills. For mentees, the program could be open to anyone interested, or you might target specific groups like new hires, recent promotions, or high-potential employees.

Match Mentors and Mentees:

The matching process is a critical step. You can allow mentees to choose their mentors, match them based on interests and goals, or use a combination of both methods. In large companies, it can be beneficial to use a software tool to assist with the matching process.

Provide Training:

Mentors will need training on how to provide effective guidance and feedback. Likewise, mentees should be prepared to take full advantage of the mentorship opportunity. Training can take the form of workshops, webinars, or even online materials.

Monitor and Adjust the Program:

Once the program is underway, it's important to monitor its progress and get feedback from the participants. This will allow you to see if the program is meeting its objectives and make any necessary adjustments.

Recognise and Reward Participation:

Mentors are typically volunteering their time, so it's essential to acknowledge their efforts. This could be in the form of public recognition, small rewards, or even just a sincere thank you.

Remember, the key to a successful mentorship program is commitment and patience. It might take time to see the results, but the long-term benefits for your employees and your organisation can be substantial.

Use Case Summary/Key Takeaways

1. Learning and Development (L&D) is a pivotal function within an organisation, and AI-powered tools like ChatGPT can significantly contribute to the planning and management of L&D programmes.

2. ChatGPT can help identify skills gaps within the organisation, suggest relevant courses and skills for different roles, and even aid in setting objectives aligned with the company's strategic goals.

3. When formulating the structure and content of the L&D programme, ChatGPT can serve as a research tool, developing a comprehensive learning programme for various roles within the organisation.

4. ChatGPT can be utilised to create relevant learning materials, such as course outlines and tests, supporting the learning objectives and enhancing the overall learning experience.

5. Implementing an L&D programme is made smoother with ChatGPT, helping in drafting communications about the programme and facilitating its launch across the organisation.

6. ChatGPT can assist in evaluating the effectiveness of the L&D programme by designing questionnaires for feedback and analysing the results to offer insights and improvements.

7. The AI-powered tool is also capable of making necessary adjustments to the L&D programme based on evaluation data, continually improving its effectiveness.

8. Lastly, ChatGPT can support the creation of a learning-oriented environment within the organisation, suggesting ways to implement mentorship programmes or continuous professional development opportunities. By harnessing the capabilities of ChatGPT, HR professionals can optimise their L&D programmes, ensure targeted skill development, and foster a culture of continuous learning and growth within their organisation.

Use Case 5 – Policy Development and Refinement

HR policies are vital to an organisation as they establish guidelines and procedures that ensure consistency, fairness, and compliance within the workforce. These policies play a crucial role in maintaining a productive and harmonious work environment while protecting the rights and interests of both the employees and the organisation. What I've found in many organisations is that policies tend to be written in the language that is relevant to the author but not necessarily to the end users. The clearer your policies are, the more effective they will be.

We'll go through three examples: (1) creating a policy from scratch, (2) analysing an existing policy, and (3) refining an existing policy to be clearer.

1. Creating a policy from scratch

Example starting prompt: "Write me a comprehensive social media policy that is easy to understand"

2. Analysing an existing policy

I've taken the example of a publicly available and current policy for a global, very well-known brand and will include it in my next prompt for analysis

Example analysis prompt: "I will provide you with our social media policy. Analyse it and suggest areas for improvement" + [paste policy text here]

ChatGPT response:

Overall, the social media policy provides a comprehensive framework for associates' behaviour and engagement on online platforms. However, there are a few areas where the policy could be improved:

1. *Update the policy: The policy is dated December 15, 2011. Given that the current date is 2023, it is crucial to update the policy to reflect the latest practices, platforms, and technologies in social media. A policy that is over a decade old may not adequately address emerging challenges and opportunities in the digital landscape.*

2. *Include guidelines on content creation: The policy emphasises the importance of representing the company positively but lacks specific guidelines on content creation. It would be beneficial to*

provide instructions on creating engaging, accurate, and compelling content that aligns with the company's values and messaging.

3. *Incorporate guidelines for crisis management: While the policy mentions negative posts and deferring to subject matter experts, it does not provide clear instructions on how to handle online crises. Including guidelines for managing and responding to crises in social media can help associates understand their role in mitigating reputational damage and maintaining transparency during challenging situations.*

4. *Expand privacy guidelines: The policy briefly mentions protecting consumers' privacy but does not provide detailed instructions on how to handle personal data, data breaches, and compliance with privacy regulations. Strengthening the privacy guidelines will help associates navigate the intricacies of handling personal information in the online space.*

5. *Address employee advocacy: The policy mainly focuses on associates representing the company officially but does not explicitly address employee advocacy or personal branding. Including guidelines on how associates can engage as brand advocates and establish their personal online presence while adhering to the company's values would be valuable.*

6. *Provide training and ongoing education: The policy mentions a Social Media Certification Program but does not elaborate on its content or availability. It would be beneficial to provide detailed information about training programs, workshops, and ongoing education initiatives to ensure that associates stay updated on best practices, industry trends, and platform-specific guidelines.*

7. *Simplify language and enhance readability: Some sections of the policy are quite dense and could be challenging for associates to understand and apply. Simplifying the language and breaking down complex concepts into actionable steps would make the policy more accessible and user-friendly.*

8. Establish a feedback mechanism: The policy does not mention a formal feedback mechanism for associates to seek clarification or report potential issues. Implementing a process for associates to ask questions, provide feedback, and report concerns related to social media activities would foster a culture of open communication and continuous improvement.

Regularly reviewing and updating the social media policy in line with industry trends and feedback from associates will help ensure its effectiveness and relevance in guiding online behaviour and brand representation.

3. Refining an existing policy to be clearer

Example analysis prompt: *"I will provide you with our employee code of conduct. Rewrite it to be more succinct and at the level that a high school graduate could easily understand"* + *[paste code of conduct text here]*

If your industry has specific requirements, it is essential to include relevant information about your industry within the prompts. For instance, the code of conduct for an educational institution will likely differ significantly from that of a mining company.

By incorporating these three types of prompts into your policies, you will guarantee their comprehensiveness and clarity.

Use Case Summary/Key Takeaways

1. HR policies act as fundamental guidelines that ensure consistency, fairness, and compliance in the workforce, fostering a productive work environment while safeguarding the interests of employees and the organisation.

2. The language and clarity of HR policies directly impact their effectiveness. Policies should be written in a language that is comprehensive to end-users, ensuring they are understood and followed properly.

3. Three types of prompts can help create, analyse, and refine policies: (1) a starting prompt to generate a new policy, (2) an analysis prompt to review and improve existing policies, and (3) a refinement prompt to make existing policies clearer and more concise.

4. ChatGPT's capability can be harnessed to create a comprehensive social media policy from scratch, demonstrating the AI's potential in generating effective HR policies.

5. When analysing an existing policy, ChatGPT can identify potential areas for improvement, including the need for updates, specific guidelines for different aspects of social media, the handling of privacy, and crisis management procedures.

6. The refinement of an existing policy involves rewriting it in a simpler, more succinct language, enhancing its readability and comprehension for all employees. AI models like ChatGPT can be helpful in translating complex policies into easily understandable text.

7. Tailoring the prompts based on industry-specific requirements can ensure the policies' applicability and relevancy.

8. Regular review and updating of HR policies, facilitated by AI, can help maintain their effectiveness and alignment with current industry trends and feedback from employees.

In the next chapter you will learn about the risks of using ChatGPT and the steps you can take to mitigate them.

6 THE RISKS OF USING CHATGPT (AND HOW TO COMBAT THEM)

In this chapter, you will learn:

- The phenomenon of "hallucination" in AI language models, its implications and mitigation strategies.

- The limitations of ChatGPT's knowledge on recent events and how to supplement it with other tools like Google's Bard chat.

- The concept of bias in AI models, how it can impact HR processes, and measures to prevent its negative effects.

- The potential data security risks associated with using ChatGPT, along with precautionary measures to protect sensitive data.

- Strategies to foster transparency, accountability, and responsibility in AI use, and the significance of building an ethical AI culture in HR.

Inaccuracies and Ambiguities: One of the biggest criticisms and limitations of ChatGPT is that it sometimes tends to produce texts that sound plausible or convincing but are incorrect or nonsensical under the surface. This phenomenon is called "hallucination" and it is common in language models. You are the expert in your area and in your specific context so it's crucial to fact check and treat ChatGPT's responses as a starting point rather than a complete answer to your question.

Limited Knowledge of Recent Events: ChatGPT, as of the book's writing, may lack knowledge in certain specialised domains or subjects since its training data only goes up until the beginning of 2022 (for the free version, April 2023 in the Plus version). However, OpenAI is currently testing a feature to include current web sources in its responses. In the meantime, if you need the latest information, an alternative is Google's Bard chat. While it may not be as proficient as ChatGPT for most of the topics covered in this book, it does offer up-to-date information that can complement the capabilities of ChatGPT.

Bias: ChatGPT is trained on a massive dataset of text, which may contain biases. This could lead to ChatGPT generating biased responses, which could have negative consequences for HR processes such as hiring and promotion.

Data Security: There are **two** main risks associated with data in your ChatGPT prompts:

1. Sensitive data in your prompts being accessed by hackers.

Mitigation 1: don't use your work email address to sign up for ChatGPT so that prompt data cannot be associated with your company and use a secure, unique password.

Mitigation 2: in ChatGPT data settings you can disable chat history which means that there's nothing for a hacker to see should they get into your account.

2. Sensitive data in your prompts being included in the ChatGPT dataset for others to access with their prompts.

Mitigation 1: don't enter company intellectual property or any personally identifiable data into your prompts.
Mitigation 2: in Settings>> Data Controls in ChatGPT, switch off the setting for "Chat History & Training" which will prevent your data from going into the model.

Transparency, accountability, and responsibility are crucial in ensuring ethical AI use. HR professionals must understand how ChatGPT works, the data it uses, and the decisions it makes to ensure accountability and responsibility in AI use. They must also be transparent with employees about how AI is being used and provide a clear explanation of how it affects their work.

To foster a culture of ethical AI use, HR professionals can start by developing guidelines and policies for AI use that align with ethical standards and principles. They should also provide regular training and education to employees on AI use and its ethical implications.

Overall, the use of ChatGPT in HR can have numerous benefits, including improved efficiency and productivity in various HR functions. Still, it also has risks relating to algorithmic bias and reducing personal touch, requiring ethical considerations to make sure it is used responsibly and with end-users and employee's best interests in mind.

Chapter Summary/Key Takeaways

1. ChatGPT can occasionally produce misleading or incorrect text, known as 'hallucination'. Users should check the facts in its responses, viewing them as starting points, not definitive answers.

2. The model's training only includes data up until the beginning of 2022 (in the free version, April 2023 in the Plus version), so it may lack recent or specialist subject knowledge.

3. If training data contain biases, ChatGPT may generate biased responses. This could negatively influence HR processes such as recruitment and promotion. Users must be aware of and address possible bias.

4. Data security is crucial when using ChatGPT. There are risks of sensitive data in prompts being accessed by hackers or included in the ChatGPT dataset.

5. Risk mitigation strategies include using a non-work email to sign up, using a unique secure password, refraining from inputting sensitive company or personal data into prompts, and disabling chat history and "Chat History & Training" in the settings.

6. Ethical AI use requires transparency, accountability, and responsibility. HR professionals should understand ChatGPT's workings, inform employees about AI usage in their roles, and oversee AI's decisions.

7. HR departments should establish ethical AI usage guidelines and regularly train staff about AI use and its ethical implications.

8. While ChatGPT can enhance HR efficiency and productivity, ethical considerations are essential to manage potential algorithmic bias and avoid lessening the personal touch in HR. AI use should prioritise the best interests of end-users and employees.

EPILOGUE

As we conclude this book, it is clear that OpenAI's ChatGPT represents a remarkable advancement in artificial intelligence. It has the potential to significantly transform various sectors, including human resources. Its capacity for generating human-like responses, sustaining coherent conversations, and performing diverse tasks makes it a crucial tool for enhancing HR processes, improving onboarding experiences, aiding performance evaluations, and advancing learning and development strategies..

Like any advanced technology, it is crucial to recognise and manage any potential risks and drawbacks associated with its use. These could include the generation of inaccurate or biased responses, data security issues, and a potential reduction in the personal touch within HR processes. To mitigate these risks, responses from ChatGPT should be viewed as preliminary guidance rather than final solutions, sensitive data should be cautiously handled, and clear guidelines for ethical AI use should be established. Transparency, accountability, and responsibility must be central to any AI implementation. HR professionals need to comprehend how ChatGPT functions, clearly communicate to employees the role of AI in their tasks, and consistently oversee AI decisions. Regular training on the ethical use of AI should be an integral part of employee training programs.

Despite the challenges, ChatGPT offers significant potential benefits. As we further explore its capabilities, we anticipate further technological advancements and applications. This transformative technology impacts not only HR and learning development but also broadens to include various facets of our professional and personal lives. The future of AI, represented by ChatGPT, is thrilling and holds promise, contingent upon our cautious, conscientious, and ethically responsible engagement.

To derive maximum value from ChatGPT, start by exploring and testing its capabilities. Consider setting it as your browser's homepage as a constant reminder of its supportive role. Challenge its limits and explore how it can transform the way you work. Remember, this is merely the beginning of an incredible journey with ChatGPT and AI, one that will reshape the landscape of human resources and how we work.

APPENDIX – CHATGPT FREE VERSUS CHATGPT PLUS

It's important to understand the differences between the Free version of ChatGPT and the ChatGPT Plus service (at time of publishing, costs USD20 per month for a license). This appendix provides a comparison, helping you make a choice that best fits your professional needs.

Understanding ChatGPT Free Version
ChatGPT Free is an accessible tool offering the foundational features of the ChatGPT model at no cost. Its key aspects include:

- **Basic Interaction Capabilities**: Ideal for automating responses to routine queries, drafting emails, and generating simple reports.

- **Standard Response Time**: Sufficient for managing non-urgent HR tasks.
- **Usage Limits**: Suitable for individual professionals handling a moderate volume of interactions.

Advantages of ChatGPT Plus
ChatGPT Plus, a subscription-based version, offers enhanced capabilities:

- **Access to GPT4 and GPT 3.5:** A significant upgrade, GPT4 excels in complex problem-solving, a notable improvement from its predecessor.

- **Advanced Reasoning:** GPT4 uses "Chain-of-Thought" prompting to simplify complex tasks, aiding in more intricate problem-solving.

- **Reliability:** GPT4 provides more reliable responses compared to earlier versions, reducing the likelihood of irrelevant or inaccurate information.

- **Expanded Word Limit:** Capable of handling over 25,000 words, facilitating the creation of in-depth HR reports and analyses.

- **Bing Search and Plugins**: Offers real-time information access, crucial for up-to-date HR information (for example being able to research current legislation).

- **Faster Response Times:** Plus users experience quicker replies and uninterrupted access, even during peak times.

Selecting the Right Version

Your choice between ChatGPT Free and Plus should consider:

- **Scale of Your Role**: The free version may be adequate for individual HR consultants or those in smaller firms. ChatGPT Plus suits HR roles in larger companies or those requiring extensive use of AI.

- **Budget Constraints**: If cost is a concern, the free version is a practical choice.

- **Response Time Necessity**: Plus is better for roles demanding quick interaction and turnaround.

- **Staying Ahead**: For professionals keen on utilising cutting-edge AI tools, Plus offers early access to new advancements.

If your company has subscribed to ChatGPT Team or Enterprise editions, this is effectively ChatGPT Plus for multiple users in an organisation.

Conclusion

The decision between ChatGPT Free and ChatGPT Plus is contingent on your specific professional requirements. While the free version caters to basic functionalities suitable for individual practitioners or small-scale roles, ChatGPT Plus offers advanced features that align with the needs of HR professionals in larger organisations or those seeking higher efficiency and advanced AI tools. Your choice should reflect your professional scale, budgetary limits, and aspiration to integrate the latest in HR technology.

ABOUT THE AUTHOR

The author, Matt Dunn, is a technology and operations improvement consultant who has led project teams to deliver operational efficiencies equating to over half a billion dollars over the course of his career.

He has a bachelor's degree in commerce and post-graduate studies in programming. His career started with data analytics and mobile technology research for the International Data from which he moved into management consulting in Europe and Australia.

In the last decade, his focus has been on improving client organisations' efficiency through the use of smart automation technology. He currently leads the automation and AI practice at a Sydney-based IT and cybersecurity company. As part of this role, he researches the latest developments in AI and automation technology and applies his findings to clients to support their digital transformation journeys. He has spoken at numerous conferences on these topics and has trained.

He lives in Kiama with his wife Nerida and their two young children, Daisy and Matilda.

ACKNOWLEDGMENTS

In the journey of writing this book, a labor of love that brimmed over with learning, challenges, and growth, I was blessed to have an army of support. I am grateful beyond words to those who accompanied me on this arduous yet rewarding venture.

To my incredible wife, Nerida, for joining me in my fascination with this technology and sending me new information as you find it. The articles and podcasts you sent my way helped me to keep up to date and, in many ways, added to the content of this book. I am eternally thankful for your support.

To my daughters, Daisy and Matilda, who put up with me harping on about this groundbreaking technology. I recall waking Daisy up to share the thrill of my first interaction with generative AI while working on an article, and she was excited about how excited I was.

My thanks to those who were my test readers and offered invaluable feedback on the draft versions of this book. My sisters, Debs, Jules, and Jacs, you've been my sounding boards, my critics, and my cheerleaders. Your insights and perspectives helped to shape the narrative, ensuring it was not only accurate but relatable and engaging.

To David McMurray, your constructive critiques, sharp observations, and immense support have been an integral part of this writing process. You've helped refine my thoughts, and for that, I am deeply appreciative.

To the nearly 2,000 people who've been in my ChatGPT training workshops, your questions during our workshops and our continued conversations have been instrumental in my learning about this technology.

This book would not be what it is without the collective contributions of each of you. You all have a stake in its creation, and I am infinitely indebted to you. Thank you.

In closing, I must extend my gratitude to my digital proofreader and research associate, ChatGPT, for its invaluable assistance cannot be overlooked.

Printed in Great Britain
by Amazon